Diwali Day

Written by: Preeti Singh   Illustrated by: Harjit Bahra

Hurray! Its Diwali today.

I wish mom and dad a Happy Diwali.

We decorate our house with small lamps called diyas.

Mom makes beautiful designs on the floor called rangoli.

We pray to Goddess Laxmi to bless us with good health and happiness.

Mom tells me the Diwali story...

"Many years ago, Prince Ram rescued his wife, Sita, from an evil King Ravana. People celebrated their return home to Ayodhya by lighting lamps and fireworks. This day is celebrated as Diwali. It signifies victory of good over evil."

My friends come over for
Diwali celebrations.

Mom gives us special sweets called mithai. Yummy!

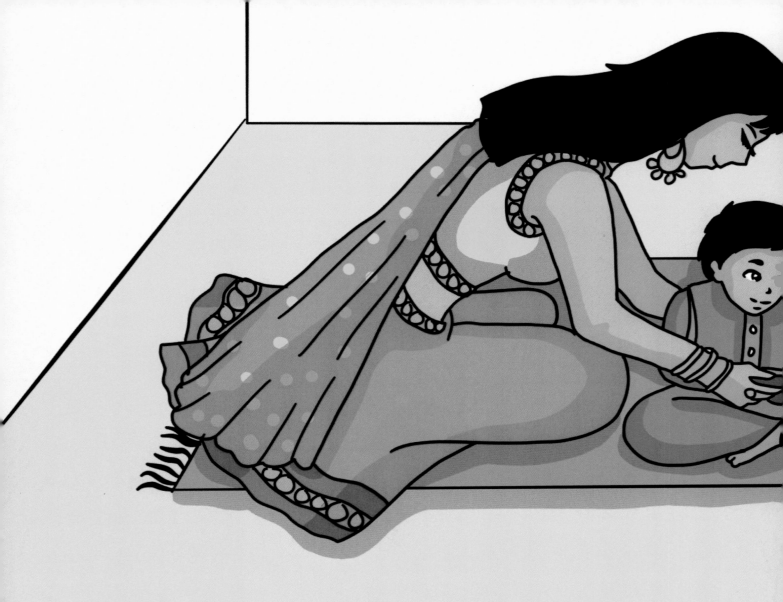

My friends and I make fun Diwali crafts!

My favorite part of Diwali is lighting sparklers and fireworks with my friends.

I love Diwali. Happy Diwali to all!

For Ahaan, the light of my life.

For Akash, who stands by me like a rock.

And for my parents, who always inspire
me to reach for the stars.

For information contact: psbookinfo@gmail.com

Designed by: Naidielee DL

ISBN: 9798683391577
Independently published

Made in the USA
Las Vegas, NV
02 November 2023